YOUR KNOWLEDGE HAS VALUE

- We will publish your bachelor's and master's thesis, essays and papers

- Your own eBook and book - sold worldwide in all relevant shops

- Earn money with each sale

Upload your text at www.GRIN.com
and publish for free

Critical Analysis of Ransomware in Relation to Cybercrime

Rhoda Kariuki

Bibliographic information published by the German National Library:

The German National Library lists this publication in the National Bibliography; detailed bibliographic data are available on the Internet at http://dnb.dnb.de.

ISBN: 9783346911629
This book is also available as an ebook.

© GRIN Publishing GmbH
Trappentreustraße 1
80339 München

Print and binding: Books on Demand GmbH, Norderstedt, Germany
Printed on acid-free paper from responsible sources.

The present work has been carefully prepared. Nevertheless, authors and publishers do not incur liability for the correctness of information, notes, links and advice as well as any printing errors.

GRIN web shop: https://www.grin.com/document/1375124

CRITICAL ANALYSIS OF RANSOMWARE IN RELATION TO CYBERCRIME.

0.0 ABSTRACT

Ransomware attacks are not a new idea, but their prevalence has risen dramatically in recent times. A key explanation for this is the financial compensation that the perpetrator stands to gain, as well as the fact that crypto-currency allows for anonymous transactions. Initially a single-host menace, ransomware is rapidly developing to conduct more sophisticated attacks by spreading through a network of hosts. One of the most difficult aspects of defending from these attacks is that every ransomware caucus is always evolving, rendering individual samples unidentifiable. Common signature-based countermeasures, such as those used to fight viruses, are made ineffective as a result. Furthermore, attempting to reverse engineer each sample in order to develop successful countermeasures or solutions is an expensive venture. Much more so now that ransomware writers are beginning to use complicated methods ensuring that getting to the original source code more difficult.

The researcher believes that a more general detection approach can be used to find a solution. It should be focused on the traits that all ransomware families share. This should help to shift the focus of research from samples to families. I collect meta-data about the files that are read and written during ransomware attacks using easy and fast metrics and applied a qualitative mode of data collection. These attacks have a common pattern of attempting to encrypt all of the victims' data. Encrypted files have a significant increase in entropy while the data size remains relatively unchanged. These characteristics can also be seen in normal user behaviour, such as when a user encrypts a file. As a result, we must allow encryption while also imposing a frequency limit to ensure that regular user traffic does not result in false positives.

Table of Contents

1.0 INTRODUCTION

Cybercrime is a by-product of the Internet's development. Cybercrime is relatively recent in comparison to traditional crime. Cybercrime, on the other hand, costs as much as traditional crime in terms of destruction. Despite the fact that cybercrime existed well before the modern computer and network, the most common definition of cybercrime is "crime involving a computer or network." To control or solve a crime, we must first comprehend its characteristics, the motives of the perpetrator, and the challenges we face.

After the advent of the modern computer and the Arpanet, we discovered the cybercrime we are familiar with, which is dependent on a network and a modern computer. Creeper, the first virus-like software, was created in 1971 by Bob Thomas, who had no intention of engaging in any illegal activity. [two] Since then, a plethora of malicious software has been created. Despite the fact that malicious software has become more complex and subtle, the primary functions and objectives have remained relatively unchanged. When we enter the Information Age, society is becoming more reliant on computers and the Internet. Despite the fact that malicious software hasn't changed much, the practice area has grown significantly. Cybercrime thrives because of the evolution of our culture.

Furthermore, traditional crime, which has been riding the wave of the Information Age, has adapted to our environment through digitalization. Drug trafficking, illicit gun trafficking, and other traditional criminal activities have begun to provide E-services, lowering the risk of being arrested. The current issue with cybercrime is that cybercriminals prey on people who are unfamiliar with computers. Aside from that, an attacker deleted a large number of evidences, making computer forensics impossible to complete. While large corporations can use various methods to ensure the security of their data logs, there is no software available for the average user. These attacks pose a serious threat, as they hold user data hostage, target network drives that might contain backup files, and attack other network hosts.

Several studies have been conducted into these types of attacks, with the most common method being to obtain a ransomware sample, execute it in a sandbox (with online connection), create a signature for the same sample, and then detect the same virus in real time. Reverse engineering a prototype to recover the original source code is another way to create a countermeasure. Both of these approaches have drawbacks. After code changes, signatures are rendered worthless, and the central command server must remain operational in order to execute the sample. Reverse engineering takes a long time and is becoming more difficult now that ransomware authors are using obfuscation techniques. Other problems arise when attempting to deploy solutions using these techniques; for example, detection software must be installed on each host, and the ransomware may target the detection software as well.

A common misconception is that a machine is always used to commit a crime. However, when a device is physically harmed by someone with malicious intent, it is often referred to as cybercrime. For example, the above-mentioned sabotage in 1820 is classified as cybercrime. Since this type of crime overlaps with causing property damage to others, it is easy for people to become perplexed.

In conclusion, my focus in this dissertation is the identification of ransomware attacks depending on the type of the communications it produces is the subject of this study, as it is the first step in developing a solution. We're looking for ransomware that targets user files stored on a network repository in particular. We want to develop a method that can detect multiple types of ransomware from various families. In the conclusions, we'll discuss which answer eventualities our solution is appropriate for. cybercrime can be described as any crime involving a device, network, or information technology.

2.0 LITERATURE REVIEW

Academics, professionals, and government agencies have all given ransomware a lot of thought all released documents with recommendations for protecting businesses from ransomware. In 2016, the FBI's Internet Crime Complaint Center issued 2,673 complaints of ransomware, resulting in reported losses of $2.4 million. In 2017, there were 1,783 ransomware reports received, resulting in an estimated $2.3 million in losses. According to the FBI (2018), the best defence against ransomware is mitigation, and it's important to take safety measures for safety. Security companies are retorting by developing advanced technological solutions to combat ransomware. Because of its prevalence, the European Union Agency for Network and Information Security (ENISA) included ransomware as a distinct threat from malware in its Cyber Threats Reports since 2016, including specific information and statistics (ENISA, 2018).

The research into the academic works found that ransomware research has exploded since 2016. Over 100 academic documents were reviewed in the databases ScienceDirect, IEEEXplore, and ACM Digital. Ransomware technical review (Subedi et al., 2018, Zimba, 2017) has strengthened our understanding of how this threat works, resulting in promising remedies. Security education policies (Simmonds, 2017), and technical controls such as detection (Jung and Won, 2018), securely-configured software and hardware (Saxena and Soni, 2018), anti-virus (AV) software (Pathak and Nanded, 2016), email security (Jakobsson, 2017), were all highlighted in the research on ransomware countermeasures (Adamov and Carlsson, 2017). Old systems should be upgraded, routine patching should be performed (Gagneja, 2017), the "least privileges" technique should be used, the network perimeter should be segregated (Fimin, 2017), and appropriate backup procedures should be implemented (Gonzalez and Hayajneh, 2017). Several recovery solutions have also been suggested to restore

(Baek et al., 2018) or decrypt (Kolodenker et al., 2017) files that were scrambled during the attack (Baek et al., 2018).

While the abundance of research on ransomware shows that academic and practitioner communities are acutely aware of the issue and eager to find appropriate solutions, the majority of the literature on ransomware, with the exception of a few exceptions, focuses solely on technological solutions (for example, Fimin, 2017, Gagneja, 2017, Richardson and North, 2017). The scholarly literature has already recognised the limitations of relying exclusively on technological solutions in the context of cyber incidents (Connolly et al., 2017a). "Security violations cannot be avoided solely by technological means," as Franke (2017, p.131) put it. Furthermore, current research emphasizes the importance of taking an interdisciplinary approach to combating cyber threats (Choo, 2014). Furthermore, despite recent technological advances (for example, antivirus software with dedicated ransomware security algorithms, advanced email filters, and so on), ransomware attacks continue to harm businesses all over the world.

Ransomware is a multidisciplinary concern, not just a technological one (Sittig and Singh, 2016). Criminals are gradually infiltrating organizational networks by employing social engineering techniques as a first point of entry. Extortion employs a variety of psychological techniques to persuade victims to pay, including countdown clocks, clear reminders of the consequences of losing data, an offer to provide security advice in order to prevent future assaults, or a strict deadline to pay with very little time to think about it. Victims are given as little as 24 hours to make a decision in some cases. Professional criminals use business models to determine the best ransom sum. Ransomware attacks are a dynamic ecosystem in which adversary actors take advantage of a variety of flaws including the 'human factor,' technological flaws, a lack of security knowledge, inadequate leadership, and insufficient funding in organizations. As a result, the aim of this research is to better understand the nature of crypto-ransomware attacks and to develop strategies that will aid organizations in responding to such incidents. We take a more holistic approach to ransomware and take a more inclusive approach to recognizing and combating this threat.

Government estimates, on the other hand, are known to understate the true rate since they depend on self-reporting. Industry studies, which publish user interactions with their antivirus products, are another source of data. Blocked detections are sometimes used as a proxy for real infections in these studies. Between June 2016 and June 2017, Symantec reported blocking 405,000 consumer ransomware infections. Though security vendor analyses have the benefit of not relying on self-reports, they are subject to other biases. Industry studies only provide insight into the experiences of a subset of the population who want to buy a security product on their own. This sample is unlikely to be representative of the general online population, since it includes people who may have a higher level of security knowledge of online threats, trust the product, and have the financial means to buy it. Furthermore, blocked detections are unreliable indicators of infection. Traditional signature-based methods can only detect and block proven threats, which means they'll miss newer attacks, whereas modern machine learning methods have a high rate of false positives.

Researchers have recently used publicly available Bitcoin transactions to estimate ransomware infections. Huang et al., for example, have a lower-bound estimate of 19,750 possible victims who paid ransom in Bitcoins around the world. They do so by scraping reports of ransomware infections from public forums and seed ransom address lists from proprietary sources that keep track of ransomware victims and their related ransom addresses, and extracting ransom addresses by running multiple ransomware binaries in a managed setting. While the presented calculation system allows for large-scale victim rate measurement, it can only provide insight into one payment process, namely Bitcoin payments.

To the best of our knowledge, no other research has been done with such a strong emphasis on crypto-ransomware. This paper focuses on crypto-ransomware since it is the most common form of ransomware today, compared to lockers and scareware, and it does the most damage due to its constant irreversibility. Furthermore, empirical studies of ransomware attacks are rarely released. Just one paper by (Shinde et al. 2016) was found in our own literature searches, in which the authors based their results on a small-sample survey and two interviews. We created a detailed collection of specific guidelines based on evidence collected directly from victims, physicians, and police.

3.0 UNDERSTANDING RANSOMWARE

This section examines the literature on ransomware, including definitions, a brief overview of how it evolved, and personal accounts from people who have been infected with the malware, as well as additional details.The aim of this information is to raise awareness and provide basic knowledge about this malware so that we can move on to the next segment, where we'll talk about the ransomware process.

3.1 Evolution of Ransomware

Since 1989, a variety of technological, economic, security, and cultural developments have had a significant impact on the evolution of ransomware (Savage, Coogan, & Lau, 2015). The first ransomware, known as AIDS Trojan or PC Cyborg, was discovered in 1989. Dr. Joseph L. Popp is the creator of this ransomware (Richardson & North, 2017). The object of PC Cyborg's development was to demand a ransom from users. This ransomware was ineffective since there were few users with personal computers at the time. Following the debacle, cyber-criminals focused their efforts on creating a more malicious ransomware that could be more easily executed (Chhillar, 2017). In 1996, Adam L. Young and Moti Yung took the initiative to introduce the first prototype asymmetric ransomware, despite the fact that the first ransomware was very useful (Gorman & McDonald, 2012). As a result, these prototype ransomwares were discovered to have some technical issues with their payment process, putting the developers at risk. As a result, the developers wanted to create a phony antivirus in order to keep their identities hidden. GPCoder, the first modern ransomware, was released in 2015. This ransomware was spread via spam email attachments posing as work applications (Richardson & North, 2017). The ransom was demanded of users who opened the attachment. Aside from that, Locker ransomware targeted users' operating systems, forcing them to pay via SMS text messages or a premium-rate phone number. During this time, cybercriminals shifted their focus from individual users to large corporations in order to extract a large ransom.

In addition, Satoshi Nakamoto created the Bitcoin payment system in order to develop payment methods. Bitcoin has since become the new payment method for online transactions. When compromised by ransomware such as CryptoLocker, CryptoWall, Virloc, and TorrentLocker, the majority of victims will pay the ransom in bitcoin. CryptoLocker is the most well-known ransomware, and it was created by a hacker called Slavik. CryptoLocker's features include encrypting and decrypting user data. This ransomware gives the victim three days to pay the ransom, which can be done with Bitcoin. The KeRanger ransomware and Xbot attacks began attacking Apple and Android users' mobile devices. This type of ransomware was risky for a large corporation like Apple because it had the potential to harm productivity and profits. KeRanger activates the files in three days and then encrypts over 300 file forms. As a result, Apple would need to release an update to stop the KeRanger ransomware.

3.2 Ransomware comes in a variety of forms.

Ransomware is the most common form of cybercrime in the world (Krunal, 2017). In general, ransomware is a form of malware that evolves like a worm and prevents or restricts users from accessing their computer by locking the screen or encrypting and locking files until a deal is completed (Deo and Farik, 2015).

There are several types of ransomware, which are divided into three categories. Crypto Ransomware, Locker Ransomware, and Hybrid Ransomware are the three basic forms of ransomware, according to (Yaqoob et al., 2017). Crypto ransomware is the first form of ransomware. Encrypting ransomware is another term for this ransomware. This ransomware employs a sophisticated algorithm to prevent users from accessing specific files. In order to decrypt the data, users must pay a ransom in bitcoins. Crypto-ransomware is a different form of ransomware that encrypts files. This ransomware is a modern ransomware that encrypts specific file types in infected systems and forces users to pay a ransom through specific online payment methods in order to receive a decrypt key (Deo & Farik, 2015).

Locker Ransomware is the second form of ransomware. Locker ransomware is a form of malware that prevents access to the target's desktop, programs, and files by locking them out of their operating systems (Shah & Farik, 2017). This ransomware differs from Crypto ransomware in that it sends out spam messages with malicious attachments to users.Users can be attacked by locker ransomware while browsing the internet or watching movies. After that, the ransomware shows a malicious message on the user's screen. The criminal would then demand a ransom payment. Winlocker is the most well-known example of Locker ransomware. Hybrid ransomware is the third kind of ransomware. This ransomware is the most offensive, as it employs every means at its disposal to increase profits. According to (Yaqoob et al., 2017), hybrid ransomware is more dangerous because it targets and disables encryption and lock mechanisms, compromising data and system functionality. Hybrid ransomware attacks can be more dangerous to users because they can threaten Internet of Things (IoT) devices and networks, as well as inflict physical harm to users before the ransom is paid.

Other forms of ransomware, such as Reveton or Police Ransomware, are also risky since they use government officers' identities. According to (Pathak et al., 2016), offenders will pose as local cops and display a warning page informing victims that they have been found doing illegal or malicious online activity and must pay a fine as a penalty.

These images have been removed due to copyright issues.

(Sample of Ransomware Note (O'Gorman & McDonald, 2012)

3.3 Phases of Ransomware

Ransomware is a new form of cybercrime that has been identified as having the potential to be extremely damaging. When hackers upload malicious software, it hinders users from using their systems before a payoff is rewarded. Ransomware mostly targets companies, and the number of victims has increased significantly in recent years. Ransomware attacks are divided into five stages (Quinkert, Holz, Hossain, Ferrara, &Lerman, 2018).

Exploitation is the initial stage of ransomware. To begin with, ransomware-infected files are normally removed from the device. Exploit kits and phishing emails are used to carry out this exploitation. It spread via email attachments and downloads as part of phishing schemes. The distribution and execution of ransomware is the second step.

This is the stage at which the ransomware executable files arrive on the victims' computers and begin the attack (Zhanhui et al., 2017). It only takes a few minutes to complete this process. In order to recover the lost data, this method will encrypt key servers. The third step of ransomware is the destruction of backup data. The ransomware would look for essential files such as JPG, Doc, and PDF in the framework. It will also look for and harm directories, including those that are hidden and contain backup files (Zhanhui et al., 2017). The aim of causing damage to the files is to discourage computer users from restoring backups.

Encryption of files is the fourth ransomware process. The goal files will be moved and renamed by criminals. After that, they'll encrypt and rename the files if the encryption is effective (Tk, 2017). When users are unable to open backup files, criminals can conduct a protected key exchange. This key will monitor the server and send commands to users. The final stage of ransomware is to alert users and demand payment. After the ransomware has erased the backup files, criminals can alert users of the payment they must make. The payment demand will be accompanied by payment instructions to remove the ransomware (Zhanhui et al., 2017). Criminals will demand payment after locking the files or device, which is typically a large sum. If the ransom is not paid within the specified period, the ransom value to decrypt the infected files is usually increased.

3.4 An attack channel for ransomware

Ransomware attacks victims or businesses through a variety of platforms. Exploit kits, malicious email attachments, and malicious email connections are all common attack methods. Exploit kits are run and malicious codes are triggered in the system when victims visit a website (Surati & Prajapati, 2017). As a result, victims will receive spam emails and notices that their computers have been locked. When a recipient opens an attachment believing it came from a trustworthy source, malicious email attachments will result (Surati & Prajapati, 2017). Victims will unwittingly open the files and download the ransomware. The device will then be compromised, and the files on it will be kept hostage.

Extortion for ransom can be used by criminals. When attacks are carried out via email links, such as URLs, the emails are sent from someone or some organizations that the victims consider to be reliable (Surati & Prajapati, 2017). Malicious files will be downloaded from the network after victims press the URL. After keeping the files hostage, the perpetrators would send a ransom notification.

As a result, ransomware can be spread via emails, apps, download operation, and exploit kits. Phishing is one of the most common and widely used methods of infecting victims' computers with malware (Singh, 2017). Criminals or attackers can create a convincing email and deliver it to their intended victims. Since malware is distributed through spear phishing, which allows criminals to gather different information about individuals or businesses, if this attack is successful, it will be considered a huge achievement for criminals. They'll use the information to intimidate victims by revealing their personal information to the media. Drive-by download victims are also at risk of being infected with ransomware. Drive-by-download is a malicious software that downloads viruses without the user's permission (Singh, 2017). Criminals are constantly on the lookout for flaws in applications or networks. This is because they want to find security flaws that they can manipulate to obtain complete access to the entire network.

3.5 The Ransomware Process

This image has been removed due to copyright issues.

Depending on the user's actions and the course taken by the criminals after receiving the ransom, the ransomware mechanism takes various paths. (Ali 2017) presented a diagram depicting the steps in the ransomware operation. The measures suggested by (Ali 2017.) in the ransomware process are as follows:

1. The machine is infected by a virus.

2. Users read the ransom note, which causes functionality to be disabled.

3. The user chooses to pay the ransom (or not)

4. The deadline has been extended.

5. The user decides to pay after the deadline has been extended.

6. Depending on whether or not it was compensated, functionality was either restored or lost for good.

4.0 Research Question

I'll now formulate our key research question and split it into many concrete sub-questions that can be solved and used to address our main question, having clarified the context and limitations of a network-based ransomware detection method in the introduction above.

We've seen that network ransomware is a hazard that existing countermeasures don't adequately address. Detecting the attack in progress is a critical step in trying to respond to a new network ransomware attack, and as previously stated, we must detect encryption by examining network traffic. The evolution of ransomware attacks and methods for diagnosing ransomware were examined in this research. This research will assist new researchers by offering summaries of previously published research works that will help them find research gaps.

"What is the evolution of ransomware attacks?" is one of the study's two concerns.

"How can you cope with the onslaught of ransomware?"

These issues are addressed by referring to a more detailed literature review of ransomware attacks from 2014 to 2018, as well as an overview of ransomware infections, which contributes to the need for ransomware preventions. As a result, we've come up with the following broad research question.

4.1 Is it possible to detect ransomware on a network that is using the samba protocol?

We'll focus on the Samba (SMB) protocol because, as previously mentioned, it's the most commonly used protocol in this setting.

Furthermore, we want to take a comprehensive approach to detecting ransomware attacks. This means we'd rather focus on detecting key ransomware activity than on the'specificities' of a particular implementation, which could change in the next version. The reason for this is that we want to make sure that the problem of analyzing and detecting ransomware samples is addressed in all families. Finally, we want this tool to be able to quickly adjust to new ransomware strains from unidentified families.

Ransomware encrypts the majority (if not all) of the files on the victim's network, which is a normal and unavoidable aspect of the attack. It will also make every effort to do so quickly in order to prevent the victim interfering with the operation. A issue with detecting such a process is the restricted time window. We're also constrained by the amount of data we have; we just have access to the information that the ransomware attack uses and provides. As a result, we'll need a method that's both fast and doesn't require a lot of information.

We assume entropy is a promising metric that can provide us with the means to detect encryption because it can describe the 'randomness' of bytes within a file by applying a series of calculations to the data itself.

5.0 METHODOLOGY

To achieve the study's aim, we used a qualitative research approach with an inductive content analysis tool as a suitable methodology. Qualitative research aims to achieve a thorough understanding of the phenomena under investigation (Maykut and Morehouse, 1994).

We conducted a series of qualitative semi-structured interviews and a focus group in order to collect rich data and gain a proper knowledge of crypto-ransomware from an interdisciplinary point of view. Our survey included people who had direct knowledge with crypto-ransomware breaches as targets or researchers, with the latter including police officers from various cybercrime units in the UK (CCU). We have used secondary data from victims, such as interview follow-up emails and confidential Incident Reports. These secondary data sources were found to be useful for post-interview clarifications and results verification in the data review. We were interested in how organizations were infected and then healed during our data collection mission. Prior to and during the attacks, we concentrated on their self-reflections, as well as any activities that helped them deter attacks and recover quickly. Finally, we looked at any lessons victims learned as a result of the attacks, as well as any post-attack organizational improvements they created. We used the information to create an all-encompassing taxonomy of crypto-ransomware countermeasures, which included a) socio-technical measures, b) front-line manager activities, and c) senior management actions. This taxonomy will serve as the foundation for a practitioner guide that will help them respond effectively to crypto-ransomware attacks. The top five countries compromised by Crypto Ransomware, according to Symantec (2016), are the United States, Canada, Japan, the United Kingdom, Italy, and Australia. Meanwhile, the United States, Germany, the United Kingdom, Russia, and China are the countries most affected by Locker Ransomware.

These images have been removed due to copyright issues.

(Top countries infected by Crypto ransomware and Locker Ransomware Source: (Symantec, 2016)

5.1 Sampling method

Twenty-six ransomware cases were chosen at random and investigated thoroughly. Between 2014 and 2018, the attacks took place. They included recently-emerged crypto-ransomware variants like Cerber, Samas, BitPaymer, WannaCry, Dharma, and HiddenTear, as well as older samples like CryptoWall, CryptoLocker, TeslaCrypt, and KeyHolder. We used a range of attack mechanisms, such as malicious emails, brute-force, and drive-by-downloads, to strike a balance between attacking humans and machines as an initial victimisation point. Our survey included businesses of different sizes and industries, as well as public and private sector organizations. The effect of ransomware attacks ranged from minor disruptions with swift recovery to major consequences that halted business operations for months.

Table 1 provides information on the attacks and the victim organizations that took part in this study. It specifies the victim's industry, size and sector of the organization, as well as the attack vector and target (human or machine). To protect the respondents' privacy, aliases are used and ransom amounts are kept hidden, since they may be used to identify some of the informants otherwise. In order to protect the respondents' privacy, the names of the ransomware variants and the dates of the events were not connected to the aliases of the organizations. These extra precautions allowed us to gain the confidence of the interviewees and collect some highly confidential information.

Table 1. A profile of respondents, organisation type and attack details.

Organisation alias	Industry; size; sector	Attack vector(s)	Attacker target
LawEnfJ	Law enforcement; small; public	Email	Human
GovSecJN	Government; large; public	Email	Human
GovSecJ	Government; large; public	Multiple attacks:	Multiple attacks:
		1.Drive-by-download	1.Machine
		2.Email	2.Human
		3.Drive-by-download	3.Machine
		4.Drive-by-download	4.Machine
EducInstF	Education; large; public	Drive-by-download	Machine
EducInstFB	Education; large; public	Brute-force	Machine
LawEnfM	Law enforcement; small	Multiple attacks:	Multiple attacks:

Organisation alias	Industry; size; sector	Attack vector(s)	Attacker target
		1.Email	1.Human
		2.Email	2.Human
GovSecA	Government; large; public	Brute force	Machine
LawEnfJU	Law enforcement; medium; public	Malicious email	Human
HealthSerJU	Health service; large; public	Multiple attacks:	Multiple attacks:
		1.Brute-force	1.Machine
		2.Malicious email	2.Human
LawEnfF	Law enforcement; medium; public	Malicious email	Human
ITOrgA	IT; small; private	Brute force	Machine
ConstrSupA	Construction; small; private	Brute force	Machine
EducOrgA	Education; small; public	Brute force	Machine
SecOrgM	IT; small; private	Email	Human

Organisation alias	Industry; size; sector	Attack vector(s)	Attacker target
ITOrgJL	IT; small; private	Brute force	Machine
CloudProvJL	IT; small; private	Brute force	Machine
InfOrgJL	Infrastructure; medium; private	Brute force	Machine
ConstrSupJ	Construction; small; private	Brute force	Machine
RelOrgJ	Religion; medium; private	Email	Human
SportClubJ	Sport; large; private	Brute force	Machine
UtilOrgD	Utilities; large; private	Brute force	Machine

6.0 RESEARCH FINDINGS

6.1 Dependability and validity

Several steps were taken to check the study's findings and ensure their reliability. The use of the purposeful sampling technique, for starters, avoided sampling distortion. Second, the sample size was calculated using the theoretical saturation theory. Third, secondary data was crucial in validating the results. Fourth, we asked respondents for input on interview transcripts and study results, and then made the necessary changes. Fifth, the findings were presented to an experienced TrendMicro researcher, who offered valuable expert feedback. Sixth, all conclusions are backed up by quotations from interviewees, which adds to the credibility. Finally, the high level of agreement among study informants about the appropriate organizational steps to react to the crypto-ransomware threat indicates that the findings are credible and unlikely to change dramatically if more organizations are surveyed. We assume that by taking these steps, we were able to remove the majority of inaccuracies and misunderstandings from the data collection process. The use of the aforementioned measures guarantees fairly consistent performance, but we do not assume that the list of proposed measures is exhaustive.

When it comes to the validity of conclusions, the problem is more complicated if the method of choice is an interview, since the interview process invariably encourages participants to answer questions in ways that misrepresent the truth. However, the situation appears to be peculiar in this research, as participants were given different incentives to provide accurate answers. While we cannot say that the study participants were completely truthful or forthcoming, a number of factors lead us to believe that the responses given by interviewees were reliable. To begin with, the majority of victims were severely harmed by crypto-ransomware attacks, which resulted in both personal emotional trauma and physical damage to IT infrastructure. Participation in this study was primarily motivated by the need to share their experiences in order to avoid potential attacks on other organizations. Many interviewees expressed genuine concern about the danger that crypto-ransomware poses, including its recent emergence and the potential implications, and some strongly objected to the fact that many businesses hide cyber-attacks. Second, some interviewees were outraged that criminals had taken them hostage and wanted to "tell their story" and warn other organizations. Third, almost all victims voluntarily engaged in validation activities and showed a strong desire to receive the final results. The very essence of the work of CCU officers is to reduce cybercrime. As a result, they have a sincere desire to provide objective evidence. We noticed that law enforcement officials readily exchanged data on ransomware attacks while carefully concealing the identity of the victims. Other strategies that could have ensured informant integrity included explicitly articulated secrecy protocols, the ability to alter or erase portions of the transcripts and this report at any time, and even the opportunity to withdraw from the study at any time.

7.0 DISCUSSION

Ransomware is becoming more popular. This is shown by the large number of ransomware attacks on high-profile companies in recent years. Because of large-scale ransomware attacks against Sony, the publication of "The Interview" was recently postponed. In the worst-case scenario, these attacks limited victims' access to their computers by encrypting, overwriting, or deleting their data. Despite the existence of malware detection systems, a device capable of specifically tracking ransomware attacks is still inaccessible. The sections that follow will delve further into ransomware protection and removal tools.

All confidential data should be saved and backed up to reduce the possibility of ransomware and to make data management easier. Making new data copies in order to recover future data is known as backing up (Brewer, 2017). Typically, attackers try to steal data, annoy data owners, and extort money in exchange for data. Data backups, on the other hand, can help mitigate risks.

Data backup eliminates the need for data owners to pay hackers because their data is already duplicated. Data that is relevant and already exists must be backed up on a regular basis. Furthermore, since it is so important to avoid infection and restore data, the backup system itself is at high risk of being a victim of ransomware attacks (Gazet, 2010). Some attackers can attempt to encrypt backups locally, so owners should use a cloud backup system or another system connected to the network only during the backup phase. Owners can create multiple data backups and recover encrypted data to reduce the risk of being attacked by ransomware.

Ransomware is often distributed by phishing attacks. The owner must exercise caution when clicking on unknown or suspect links or opening spam email attachments. Infected user emails, email attachments, and poor connections are all popular ways for ransomware to infect computers. Phishing and text messaging are examples of techniques that can be used (Allen, 2017). Criminals also used a variety of methods, including creating fake ads to entice people to click on them and inadvertently spread ransomware. Data owners can prevent malicious advertisements by using ad blockers and turning off Java and Java Script. Operating systems and security frameworks are updated on a regular basis. This step is necessary to ensure that infrastructure receives the most recent security updates and that a company's network remains secure. The revised architecture and modern protection technologies will help to reduce ransomware infections. Users should use the initial alert to detect file changes and track ransomware activity, according to Scaife (2016). Any device that has been infected with a virus should be turned off right away. Ransomware spreads across network links, shared storage, and shared passwords once infected (Collier, 2017). To prevent ransomware infections from spreading across an organization's network, machines should be removed from the network as soon as possible. Authorized staff must inspect and repair suspected infected networks until they can be connected to the network and restored to normal service. Many anti-ransomware tools are available on the market that can be used to resolve and reduce the possibility of ransomware attacks on personal computers or an organization's network infrastructure. First and foremost, Lock Screen Ransomware Tools from Trend Micro. It's designed to keep track of and remove ransomware lock-screens. This form of ransomware prevents users from accessing their computers or networks. Users are compelled to pay a fee to regain access to their files, similar to how other ransomware works.

It has two modes of operation. When the default system mode is disabled, but files can still be accessed in safe mode, for example. When the ransomware lock screen disables standard and secure operating modes, the second scenario occurs. Until rebooting the system, the tools will clean and delete infected files. The second anti-ransomware program to detect and counter malware and ransomware attacks is Avast Anti-Ransomware Tools. Not all ransomware attacks are the same or behave in the same way. Downloading, using, and detecting viruses with Avast decryptors is completely secure. It has a decryption wizard that asks for two copies of the user's files. Separate the files into two groups: password-protected and unprotected.

CTB- Locker, Locky, Petya, and Tesla Crypt Ransomware attacks can all be thwarted with BitDefender Anti-Ransomware Tools. If the program is turned on, it will detect infection by starting and stopping ransomware until it spreads to other files on the device. The program's splash screen is safe, but the infected component prevents executables from being run to specific locations, enabling boot security. The app does not replace existing anti-virus software; rather, it complements it. Kaspersky Anti-Ransomware Tools is the last choice. It was created with small and medium-sized businesses in mind (SME). It comes with software to keep computers from being infected and to shut down the entire computer network. Every day, the tools run and track network activity, looking for suspicious trends and behaviour. The tools are also appropriate for businesses because they are free, simple to use, and provide a high level of network security.

We'll begin by answering the sub-questions, then combine them to arrive at a conclusion for our research question and thesis.

Is it possible to identify encrypted file transfers via SMB using entropy-based methods? For our first sub-question, we chose entropy-based methods because we believed they would cover a wide range of ransomware detection scenarios. They are particularly useful for decrypting encrypted data. We also assumed that in order to detect ransomware in real time, they would only need limited data and would have good runtime efficiency.

We examined their theoretical and practical output and discovered that normalized entropy outperformed the others. Furthermore, we showed that when it comes to detecting encryption, 1-gram entropy outperforms 2-gram entropy. We arrived at this conclusion based on the smaller overlap of un- and encrypted files in 1-gram entropy.

An entropy-based approach would be capable of detecting coded file transfers in SMB traffic, we can deduce. Can we detect the encryption process based on entropy and data size by comparing the reading and writing of a file? For the second sub-question, rather than just looking at an encrypted file, we investigated the encryption process. High entropy was discovered to be one of the most significant characteristics, but it is not unique to encrypted data. We argued that encrypting a file's data would increase its entropy significantly, but that compression would as well. We did agree, however, that compression and encryption serve different purposes: the former aims to reduce data size, while the latter aims to secure data.

We also show how to calculate the entropy function for messages that are part of a conversation. In the same portion, this feature, along with the data size feature, is used to build the general detection process.

We conclude that we have created a solution that can detect ransomware on an SMB-enabled network in real time. This is accomplished by analyzing features extracted from emails, building exchanges, and detecting ransomware based on its basic features.Furthermore, we can distinguish between normal user traffic and malicious ransomware using behavioral analysis.

8.1 Preventive Measures

Users should provide incremental online and offline backups of all relevant data and photographs to prevent their data from being unrecoverable. Furthermore, all of the built-in defense mechanisms and detection tools should be kept operational at all times. Threat exposure can be reduced as much as possible using common sense, web or IP address blocking, and endpoint security. Anti-virus, firewalls, intrusion prevention systems, and web and mail filtering can all be used to ensure that an organization's or individual's electronic security is as strong as possible. Organizations should implement policies that discourage infiltration by ensuring proper system configuration and software 'hardening.' It is essential to incorporate a comprehensive and gradual back-up system for business and personal-critical information. Personnel must also ensure that offline backups are kept offline at all times to ensure that they are secure. To ensure protection, backups should be checked on a regular basis. Organizations should implement strong policies and procedures, as well as a practical framework for educating users about how to better avoid and respond to ransomware attacks. Users should implement a general information policy defining which websites are Safe for Work (SFW) and which are Not Safe for Work (NSFW), as well as educate themselves and their teams on the threats and methods used to cause ransomware and carry out attacks from start to finish. To avoid falling victim to rapidly changing and adapting ransomware attacks, organizations must have a framework in place that searches for anomalous activities such as rapid encryption or malicious non-human activity. The position of data on file systems, especially in unstructured formats such as documents, presentations, and spreadsheets, should be known. Personal data access should be restricted to those who have a need-to-know basis or by role-based access controls. The aim is to make it impossible for attackers to gain access to sensitive information after hacking an ordinary user – for example, via a phishing email – and launching ransomware using that user's credentials. To further reduce the attack surface, organizations can delete and/or archive obsolete or stale personal data. Ordinary users, whose credentials are being used by the ransomware, should not conduct large-scale file system crawls, browsing via each directory, and inspecting files. As a result, monitoring software, particularly that based on User Behaviour Analytics (UBA), should be able to detect the ransomware and restrict the number of files encrypted. Companies should back up their file systems on a regular basis, particularly important and sensitive data, and have a plan in place to restore the data in the event of a cyber-attack.

8.2 Email etiquette

Following steps implemented after a user opened a malicious email and compromised the network. Certain connections and attachments were blocked, and identifiers were added to the headers of emails sent from outside sources. Similarly, checking suspicious emails with a malicious code review tool. While email hygiene will not prevent every malicious email, the majority of them will be filtered out, according to the respondents. Email is the most popular source of ransomware infections, according to Mohurle and Patil (2017), so filters must be introduced to prevent malicious emails from reaching users' inboxes. Even if an email appears to come from an authentic recipient, Prakash et al. (2017) recommended manual scanning of emails containing links and attachments. Prakash et al. (2017) pointed out that attackers can easily spoof an email address to deceive users as to the source when discussing Locky attacks. However, in today's workplaces, workers are often under pressure to meet deadlines, so they may not have the time to double-check an email that appears to be valid and will instead click on a connection or attachment. As a result, businesses should presume that any malicious email that reaches an employee's inbox will be opened, and prepare to take effective countermeasures. As a result, relying solely on email hygiene to protect organizations from crypto-ransomware is ineffective, and additional technological steps are needed.

8.3 Advanced monitoring and recognition

According to our respondents, insufficient or absent monitoring and security measures, such as antivirus software and firewalls, is responsible for many ransomware attacks. Since learning from their mistakes, they implemented advanced antivirus software and switched to a cloud-based model for centrally managed security updates. Changing from a signature-based to a behavior-based antivirus solution is also an option. Advanced monitoring and detection software has also been installed, which proactively feeds information about emerging threats and alerts businesses, allowing them to take action before attack campaigns begin. Additionally, upgraded firewalls and applications that can detect and block malicious IPs when ransomware tries to connect back to the control server have been enabled, providing a higher level of protection.

The primary objectives of antivirus software are malware prevention, identification, and elimination. It must, at the very least, provide a higher level of protection than signature-based protection in order to detect unknown threats. Antivirus software, on the other hand, is not all produced equal. According to Al-rimy et al. (2018), advanced detection systems are still vulnerable, and ransomware may still go undetected on a network. According to Sukwong et al., users should exercise caution before downloading or opening any unknown files (2011). According to Kaspersky, the benefits of cloud-based antivirus over locally controlled antivirus include automatic updates and a lower processing power requirement to keep the computer safe (2018). Despite the fact that the effectiveness of several leading security vendors' anti-virus solutions with dedicated ransomware protection is questionable,

Firewalls filter incoming traffic and can be configured to allow or block packets from specific IP addresses and ports. Modern firewalls, according to Sophos (2017), can effectively defend against ransomware attacks. For example, a sophisticated firewall may include an Intrusion

Detection System (IDS) that performs deep packet inspection to prevent attacks like WannaCry and NotPetya, as well as blocking network exploits like EternalBlue. Furthermore, the IDS will detect connections with malicious IP addresses and instruct routers to terminate those connections. Sandboxing technology, which detects abnormal files at the gateway and moves them to a safe location for behavioral analysis, may be provided by a firewall to assist a user at the network entry. Sadaoui et al. (2014), on the other hand, cautioned that firewall effectiveness is largely dependent on configuration consistency, necessitating a systematic approach to firewall management. Firewall maintenance, in general, necessitates a high level of technical knowledge. Moore (2010) also warned that a firewall is just one tool in a wider cyber security toolkit, and that it is not the only response to security threats. Though research into detection technologies is ongoing and promising, businesses should not rely solely on detection technologies to protect themselves from crypto-ransomware.

8.4 Disaster recovery and backups

Backups have been emphasized in academic literature (Kumar and Kumar, 2013), as they are the only true line of technical defense against crypto-ransomware (after the infection takes place). Backups must be current, checked on a regular basis, and stored in places that are inaccessible to ransomware (Al-rimy et al., 2018). Maintaining backups in larger networks is more difficult, and having a consistent recovery plan is important.

9.0 CONCLUSION

When dealing with ransomware infections, there are several challenges to tackle (Singh Rajput, 2017). Many ransomware attacks forced the resetting of Internet of Things (IoT) devices that had become unusable due to previous attacks, leaving the owner with no choice but to pay the ransom. As a result, the first step in resolving this issue is to identify the device and perform inspections until it is identified. During a previous ransomware attack, the machines were unable to upload extensions or other files with a specific name as an identifier. IoT device protection and design, as well as uniform operating systems, communications, networks, data, and sensors, are all major challenges. If full security is to be extended to IoT systems, ransomware must not be compromised during the application lifecycle. Furthermore, IoT devices can only perform functions, monitor, control, and rearrange themselves within the network.

Over the next few years, it's fair to expect ransomware to grow. If ransomware is not taken seriously, it can not only disable entire business networks, but it can also disable an entire city or even a country before the demanded ransom is paid. Cyber criminals who want to disable ecosystems rather than just the network are likely to target industrial control systems (ICS) and other critical infrastructure. One of the few targets that cyber criminals might be after is payment networks like Ebay. In a transit attack in 2016, ransomware was used to hack a service provider's kiosk.

Ransomware has also infected hospitals and transportation firms. According to conventional wisdom, cryptocurrencies will fuel the growth of ransomware, but our findings show that most cases in 2016–2017 were not solely dependent on cryptocurrency for payment. Another open question for future research is whether payment rates will rise or fall as more people are infected, either because they have been victims of ransomware before or because they have learned more about it from affected friends and family. Further research could look at what factors influence payment rates in greater depth, as well as how users view their vulnerability to attack, what influences their risk thresholds, whether they are well-calibrated, and how previous infections influence their perceptions.

In principle, vulnerability can be inferred from self-reported security behaviors and past exposure to online scams, according to the clear approach to risk assessment that we present.

Assailants may be able to strike broader targets in the future, such as industrial robots used in production or infrastructure sectors that link smart cities. Extensions via the internet are regarded as attached because the online network, which includes smart devices and vital infrastructure, is extremely vulnerable and easy to attack. Cyber criminals will continue to create, launch, and benefit from this cybercrime threat in the future.

10.0 REFERENCES

Adamov, A., & Carlsson, A. (2017, September). The state of ransomware. Trends and mitigation techniques. In *2017 IEEE East-West Design & Test Symposium (EWDTS)* (pp. 1-8). IEEE.

Ali, A. (2017). Ransomware: a Research and a Personal Case Study of Dealing With This Nasty Malware. Issues in Informing Science & Information Technology, 14, 87–99. https://doi.org/10.1080/13880290490480167

Baek, S., Jung, Y., Mohaisen, A., Lee, S., & Nyang, D. (2018, July). SSD-insider: Internal defense of solid-state drive against ransomware with perfect data recovery. In *2018 IEEE 38th International Conference on Distributed Computing Systems (ICDCS)* (pp. 875-884). IEEE.

Choo, K. K. R. (2014). A conceptual interdisciplinary plug-and-play cyber security framework. In *ICTs and the Millennium Development Goals* (pp. 81-99). Springer, Boston, MA.

Connolly, L. Y., Lang, M., Gathegi, J., & Tygar, D. J. (2017). Organisational culture, procedural countermeasures, and employee security behaviour. *Information & Computer Security*.

Deo, S., &Farik, M. (2015). Information Security-Recent Attacks In Fiji. International Journal of Scientific & Technology Research, 4(8), 218-220.

European Union Agency for Network and Information Security [ENISA] 2018
European Union Agency for Network and Information Security [ENISA] (2018) "Top 15 cyber threats in 2017", ENISA. [Online] Available: [Accessed October 2018]https://www.enisa.europa.eu/topics/csirts-in-europe/glossary/ransomware.
Fimin, M. (2017). Are employees part of the ransomware problem?. *Computer Fraud & Security*, 2017(8), 15-17.

Franke, U. (2017). The cyber insurance market in Sweden. *Computers & Security*, 68, 130-144.

Gagneja, K. K. (2017, February). Knowing the ransomware and building defense against it-specific to healthcare institutes. In *2017 Third International Conference on Mobile and Secure Services (MobiSecServ)* (pp. 1-5). IEEE.

Gonzalez, D., & Hayajneh, T. (2017, October). Detection and prevention of crypto-ransomware. In *2017 IEEE 8th Annual Ubiquitous Computing, Electronics and Mobile Communication Conference (UEMCON)* (pp. 472-478). IEEE.

Jakobsson, M. (2017, April). Short paper: addressing sophisticated email attacks. In *International Conference on Financial Cryptography and Data Security* (pp. 310-317). Springer, Cham.

Jung, S., & Won, Y. (2018). Ransomware detection method based on context-aware entropy analysis. *Soft Computing, 22*(20), 6731-6740.

Kolodenker, E., Koch, W., Stringhini, G., & Egele, M. (2017, April). Paybreak: Defense against cryptographic ransomware. In *Proceedings of the 2017 ACM on Asia Conference on Computer and Communications Security* (pp. 599-611).

Krunal, G. (2017). Survey on Ransomware: A New Era of Cyber Attack. International Journal of Computer Applications, 168(3), 975–8887. Retrieved from https://pdfs.semanticscholar.org/71df/288033380d3023f09d49b7b55a77677d27a2.pdf

O'Gorman, G., & McDonald, G. (2012). Ransomware: A growing menace. Symantec Corporation.

Pathak, P. B., & Nanded, Y. M. (2016). A dangerous trend of cybercrime: ransomware growing challenge. *International Journal of Advanced Research in Computer Engineering & Technology (IJARCET), 5*(2), 371-373.

Pathak, P. B., &Nanded, Y. M. (2016). A Dangerous Trend of Cybercrime: Ransomware Growing Challenge. International Journal of Advanced Research in Computer Engineering & Technology, 5(2), 371–373. Retrieved from http://ijarcet.org/wp-content/uploads/IJARCET-VOL-5-ISSUE-2-371-373.pdf

Quinkert, F., Holz, T., Hossain, K. S. M., Ferrara, E., &Lerman, K. (2018). RAPTOR: Ransomware Attack PredicTOR. arXiv preprint arXiv:1803.01598.

Richardson, R., & North, M. M. (2017). Ransomware: Evolution, mitigation and prevention. *International Management Review, 13*(1), 10.

Saxena, S., & Soni, H. K. (2018, February). Strategies for ransomware removal and prevention. In *2018 Fourth International Conference on Advances in Electrical, Electronics, Information, Communication and Bio-Informatics (AEEICB)* (pp. 1-4). IEEE.

Shah, N., &Farik, M. (2017). Ransomware - Threats Vulnerabilities And Recommendations. International Journal of Scientific & Technology Research, Vol 06, Iss 06, Pp 307-309 (2017) VO - 06, 6(6), 307–309.

Shinde, R., Van der Veeken, P., Van Schooten, S., & van den Berg, J. (2016, December). Ransomware: Studying transfer and mitigation. In *2016 International Conference on Computing, Analytics and Security Trends (CAST)* (pp. 90-95). IEEE.

Simmonds, M. (2017). How businesses can navigate the growing tide of ransomware attacks. *Computer Fraud & Security, 2017*(3), 9-12.

Singh, -Abhaypratap. (2017). Ransomeware : A high profile attack Abhaypratapsingh. International Research Journal of Engineering and Technology(IRJET), 4(2), 1854–1859. Retrieved from https://irjet.net/archives/V4/i2/IRJETV4I2365.pdf

Sittig, D. F., & Singh, H. (2016). A socio-technical approach to preventing, mitigating, and recovering from ransomware attacks. *Applied clinical informatics, 7*(2), 624.

Subedi, K. P., Budhathoki, D. R., & Dasgupta, D. (2018, May). Forensic analysis of ransomware families using static and dynamic analysis. In *2018 IEEE Security and Privacy Workshops (SPW)* (pp. 180-185). IEEE.

Surati, S. B., &Prajapati, G. I. (2017). A Review on Ransomware Detection & Prevention. International Journal of Research and Scientific Innovation Issue IX, IV(Ix), 2321–2705. Retrieved from http://www.rsisinternational.org/IJRSI/Issue46/86-91.pdf

Tk, A. (2017). Discussion On Ransomware ,WannacryRansomware and Cloud Storage Services Against Ransom Malware Attacks, 2(6), 310–314.

Yaqoob, I., Ahmed, E., Hashem, I. A. T., Ahmed, A. I. A., Gani, A., Imran, M., &Guizani, M. (2017). Internet of things architecture: Recent advances, taxonomy, requirements, and open challenges. IEEE wireless communications, 24(3), 10-16.

Zhanhui, L., Azlina, N., & Rahman, A. (2017). A Review on Ransomware Trend of Attacks and Prevention, 12(16), 6201–6210

Zimba, A. (2017). Malware-free intrusion: a novel approach to ransomware infection vectors. *International Journal of Computer Science and Information Security*, *15*(2), 317.

YOUR KNOWLEDGE HAS VALUE

- We will publish your bachelor's and master's thesis, essays and papers

- Your own eBook and book - sold worldwide in all relevant shops

- Earn money with each sale

Upload your text at www.GRIN.com and publish for free